YOUR KNOWLEDGE HAS VALUE

- We will publish your bachelor's and master's thesis, essays and papers

- Your own eBook and book -
  sold worldwide in all relevant shops

- Earn money with each sale

Upload your text at www.GRIN.com
and publish for free

Bibliographic information published by the German National Library:

The German National Library lists this publication in the National Bibliography; detailed bibliographic data are available on the Internet at http://dnb.dnb.de .

This book is copyright material and must not be copied, reproduced, transferred, distributed, leased, licensed or publicly performed or used in any way except as specifically permitted in writing by the publishers, as allowed under the terms and conditions under which it was purchased or as strictly permitted by applicable copyright law. Any unauthorized distribution or use of this text may be a direct infringement of the author s and publisher s rights and those responsible may be liable in law accordingly.

Imprint:

Copyright © 2012 GRIN Verlag, Open Publishing GmbH
Print and binding: Books on Demand GmbH, Norderstedt Germany
ISBN: 978-3-668-10501-0

This book at GRIN:

http://www.grin.com/en/e-book/311753/marx-and-weber-s-concept-of-capitalism

Alina Degtiarova

Marx' and Weber's Concept of 'Capitalism'

GRIN Publishing

GRIN - Your knowledge has value

Since its foundation in 1998, GRIN has specialized in publishing academic texts by students, college teachers and other academics as e-book and printed book. The website www.grin.com is an ideal platform for presenting term papers, final papers, scientific essays, dissertations and specialist books.

Visit us on the internet:

http://www.grin.com/

http://www.facebook.com/grincom

http://www.twitter.com/grin_com

Introduction	1
Weber's Understanding of Capitalism	1
Marx' Understanding of Capitalism	7
Weber and Marx Comparison	11
Conclusion	12
References	13

Introduction

Karl Marx and Max Weber are the classics of German sociology of the end of 19th and the beginning of 20th centuries. This paper provides a brief overview on Marx' and Weber's perception and definition of the notion of 'capitalism' as well as their further comparison. Capitalism in the theories of these two prominent sociologists is represented from the different points of view, thus, the comparison promises to be significant. As the main sources for this research it is planned to use main works of Karl Marx and Max Weber on capitalism, particularly: "Capital: A Critique of Political Economy" and "The Protestant Ethic and the Spirit of Capitalism" along with analytics and criticisms of their theories, which have been done by other sociologists.

Weber's understanding of 'capitalism'

Capitalism serves as one of the main topics in Max Weber's research. Though, he is especially interested not in capitalism in its traditional understanding, but in its ethical and cultural value, which represents capitalism in variety of its perspectives. For Weber, 'capitalism' is not just a notion of political economy, as it was majorly regarded before him, but cultural and sociological concept. According to Weber, a modern capitalism is an inescapable consequence of Europe's historical development and there is no way back to the patriarchal structures and values. Weber's analysis focuses on the combination of political, economic and religious structures, which were shaping the Western capitalism. The foundation of the European capitalism Weber saw in religion, particularly in Protestantism. In his work "The protestant ethic and the spirit of capitalism" Weber starts over with the denial of the perspective on capitalism as an aspiration for gaining the profit (Weber 1996). For him, this aspiration is hardly related to capitalism as it is common for people of all types and classes. Unrestrained avidity of possession is not equal to capitalism or its spirit in Weber's perspective. Capitalism does represent the desire for possession, but a very rational one. If we consider capitalism in its traditional understanding as an economic activity, which was oriented on making profit and expenses in terms of money, then in this sense, according to Weber, capitalism existed in many countries around the world. The main issue in Weber's research was the origin of the bourgeois capitalism with it rational organization of free labor.

The main idea in "The protestant ethic and the spirit of capitalism" in its approach to understand the Western capitalism is that even though the economic conditions are important in sense of rationalization of technology and rational law, the economic rationalism is dependent on the ability and people's proneness to certain types of practical and rational life behavior as well.

Weber points out the conditionality of the economic mentality and economy type by the certain religious orientation. The conditionality of the modern Western capitalism and the protestant ideology Weber proves by the various statistical data. Particularly, by the fact that the majority of the capital holders and entrepreneurs were represented by protestants, by the prevalence of protestants in the qualified classes of workers, as well as higher technological personnel in modern factories (Weber 1996: 35).

According to Weber, here it is possible can observe a certain causal relationship, connected to a certain psychology, which was cultivated by the education. In Protestantism this psychology had an orientation on the professional activity. In his point of view, one should look for the reason of different way of action of Catholics and Protestants, first of all in the stable internal originality of each confession and in their purely religious traits.

Explaining of the Protestant ethic Weber reveals the inner originality of this belief. Thus, referring to people raised in Protestantism ideology, he notes that they have a commitment to the 'duty to labor' which creates the most favorable conditions for work as understanding of vocation. That is what made the original motivational structure of the behavior of the urban European class - the bourgeoisie. This ethical core of the Protestant religion was the most adequate form of high-yield industrial capitalism. Noting the invasion of the new spirit, 'the spirit of modern capitalism' Weber does not reduce the issue of expansion of the driving forces of modern capitalism only to the question about the source of the financial resources used by the capitalist. He focuses on the distinct ethical qualities of the people who were able to provide necessary conditions for the unlimited growth in labor productivity. The formation of the ethical qualities of men of the "new type" the author of the "Protestant ethic" relates to the ideas of Martin Luther and his reform activities, in particular, the reinterpretation of the secular activities and interpretation of a professional vocation and equality of all occupations before God.

Weber points out that, "we only wish to ascertain whether and to what extent religious forces have taken part in the qualitative formation and the quantitative expansion of that [Capitalist] spirit over the world. Furthermore, what concrete aspects of our capitalistic culture can be traced to them?"(Weber 1996: 91)

Given the enormous complexity of the relationship between material basis, the forms of social and political organization and the spiritual content of the Reformation era, Weber tries, above all, to establish the link between certain points of the known forms of religious belief and professional ethics. This, in his opinion, can identify the general direction of the impact that religious movement has had on the development of the material culture. And only after it will be well established, it is possible to, according to Weber, try to determine to what extent the content of modern culture should be kept to religious grounds and to what extent to the motives of another kind.

Thus, it is possible to get the key to understanding the uniqueness of modern capitalism, as trying to understand the inside, with point of view it heralds spiritual motivation and creators - motivation, that has a moral and religious origins and impulses. Based on religious and ethical aspirations of Protestants, belonging to the ascetic wing of Protestantism, one gets to understanding of purely external "material" results of the modern capitalism. That is how Protestant religious asceticism resulted in a system of self-restraint future functionaries of modern capitalist production. It is in these religious communities, according to Weber, psychological stimuli have been created by religious belief and practice of religious life. These stimuli gave certain directions to the whole order of life and forced individual to adhere to them.

These incentives have been largely determined by the specific religious beliefs, one of which was the setting that the world exists to serve the self-glorification of God, and Christian exists only to carry out in his secular life for the glory of the commandments of God. And what is also important Christian social activity is pleasing to God, as he (God) wants the social order of life to correspond to his commandments and their goal. This applies in particular to Calvinism and the professional activity, which is part of secular life for the common good and is aimed at the rational transformation of the social world. According to the canons of Calvinism people felt like a tool of God, and no doubt in their selectness. In matters of religion Calvinistic faith determined the utilitarian character of Calvinistic ethics and a number of distinctive features of the concept of a professional calling.

By analyzing the practical ethics of Calvinism, which created consistent and rational method for the life of believer, Weber shows that the reformist transformations, carrying a specific colored ascetic, were not alien to Catholicism. The Protestant asceticism, like any other rational asceticism, sought to teach person to be guided by the constant principles (motives), but not affects, in other words, sought to bring up a personality in him. Methodical regulation of the entire man lifestyle particularly distinguishes Calvinistic asceticism, which was also forced to carry out their ascetic ideals within mundane professional activities. In the puritanical interpretation we have, according to Weber, we are dealing not just with the apotheosis of labor, but with the apotheosis of the division of labor and specialization as well. Only specialty (profession specific), according to the ideologues of English Puritanism, promotes skills of workers and leads to increase in productivity for the common good. English Puritanism covers not only the professional labor, but wealth as well. As follows from the instructions, the wealth is condemned insofar as it is fraught with the temptation to indulge in laziness inactivity and sinful worldly pleasures. Wealth as an implementation of professional duty is not only justified morally, but even prescribed. In this sense, contrary to the Catholic orthodoxy, the desire to be poor was seen as a desire to be sick, and it is reprehensible, as detrimental to the fame of God.

Thus, just as the emphasis of the ascetic value of the constant profession is an ethical idealization of modern professional specialization, so the providential interpretation of greed, according to Weber, serves the idealization of a business person. All of this in spiritual and moral terms has contributed to the fact that Puritanism became the bearer of the bourgeois ethos of business and management as well as the rational organization of labor. A worldly asceticism of Protestantism, which have rejected the direct enjoyment of wealth, however, contributed to the liberation of acquisitiveness from psychological oppression of the traditionalist ethics and broke the shackles that limited commitment to gain, making it not only lawful, but also pleasing to God. It is equally important to understand the spirit of capitalism is the conclusion by Weber that the Puritans, with their specific outlook contributed to the establishment of the bourgeois, rational lifestyle in economic terms, which, according to Weber, is infinitely more important than the mere encouragement of capital investment. Just puritanical attitude to life has been the mainstay of this trend, and Puritans - its only consistent supporters. It should be noted that this idea along with disappearance of its religious roots was given the utilitarian hue, which was the leitmotif of capitalist economy and its productivity theory, at least in its early stage of development. Namely: the need for low wages as one of the foundations productivity was postulated. No less important factor in terms of capitalist economy was the religious promotion of the individual management of the legal business based on personal qualities and personal initiative. Moreover, as Weber notes that "while the politically privileged monopoly industries in England all disappeared in a short order, this attitude played a large and decisive part in the development of the industries which grew up in spite of and against the authority of the State." (Weber 1996: 179) And it is very important here the assessment of the situation connected with the idea professional vocation from the cultural point of view - the point of perspectives of human development, which is central for modern life.

Another important factor in shaping the modern 'spirit of capitalism', concluded in Puritanism, and communities and ascetic sects based on it, is their radical break with the various patriarchal shackles and desire, on the basis of commandments, to obey God more than men. This, according to Weber, was one of the most important prerequisites of modern individualism. And in this regard, the guild organization in its medieval form, if served a premise (though contrary to its purpose) for the development of capitalism and forms of competition, but only one guild organization could not of course, give rise to the bourgeois-capitalist ethos. Individualistic impulses in the economy were caused by first of all, the living conditions of the ascetic sects.

Such, in general, according to Weber, the main directions of the religious influence and ethical norms of behavior that have emerged on the basis of Protestantism and determined the spirit of Western capitalism. This spirit with its tendency to the universal rationalization features the modern capitalism from its patriarchal form with 'irrational and speculative character'. Ascetically minded Protestant formed a functionary of the industrial ethos of the future capitalist production, with its propensity for the technological application of the scientific knowledge and the rationalization of law structure and legal state structure, which in its formal definition, according to him, and carries only the West. Here, apparently, it is necessary to recognize that the type of the attitude towards reality, which is typical for Protestantism, and that social reality that this type have been formed of, for Europe were much more versatile than expected. We can say that great importance of Weber's "Protestant Ethic and the Spirit capitalism" is that he was the first to document the importance of cultural and ethical attitudes of Protestantism for the capitalistic development of the West. In addition, it simultaneously through a comparison with Protestantism has revealed the nature of rationality as a fundamental principle of the industrial society.

Marx' understanding of 'capitalism'

As a scientist Marx proceeded simultaneously from the three scientific sources: British classical political economy of Smith and Ricardo (Marx 1990), the German classical philosophy of Hegel and the utopian Socialism (Lwith 1993: 89-95). In Smith and Ricardo he borrowed the labor theory of value, provisions of the Act of the tendency of the rate of profit to decrease, productive labor. In the second - the idea of dialectics and materialism, the third - the concept of class struggle, the elements of the sociological structure of society.

The main idea was that people in the social production of their life become part of certain necessary relations, which are independent from their will and these relations correspond to the certain stage of development of their power of the material production. The scope of these relations builds the economic structure of the society. In the social production of their life, people enter into definite relations that are indispensable and independent of their will - relations of production which correspond to a certain stage of development of their material productive forces. The combination of these relations of production constitutes the economic structure of society, the real foundation, on which a legal and political superstructure raises and to which definite forms of social consciousness correspond.

Method of production of material life stipulates the social, political and intellectual life process in general. Is not the consciousness of men that determines their being, but on the contrary, their social being that determines their consciousness.

In the concept of base and superstructure there was an attempt to give an economic interpretation of history considering the development of productive forces and relations of production, which suggests the process of transition from capitalism to socialism, as a bourgeois social formation completes the prehistory of the human society. According to Marx, non-dialectical approach, and unwarranted recognition of laws of the capitalist economy as universal, has made it not possible to understand for representatives of classical political economy, which in fact discovered the laws, that they have a specific and transient nature.

In Karl Marx' judgment, capitalism, the era of which has its origins in 16th century (Marx 1990) excludes the humanization of society and democracy because of the private ownership of the means of production and the anarchy of the market. In this system people work for profit, there is exploitation of one class by another, and people (the entrepreneur and the worker) become alien to themselves, because they cannot fulfill their potential in work, which degraded into a means of existence in an unpredictable market and stiff competition struggle. Concerning the true freedom outside of labor, i.e. free time, it is, according to Marx, will not become the measure of wealth, neither under capitalism, nor under communism. Marx introduced a number of reasons, for believing that the capitalist system will function worse and worse, but has not proved economically that the internal contradictions of capitalism will destroy it.

It should be emphasized that in Marx's arguments about the imminent collapse of Capitalism the violation of market principles of income's allocation between social classes is not the main point, but the fact that this system does not provide full employment, tends to colonial exploitation and war. He considers socialism and communism as a social ideal, calling them phases of non-antagonistic communist society in which means of production will no longer be the subject of individual appropriation and man will find freedom.

However, Marx's belief in the triumph of the ideals of a classless society is based primarily on the class theory. Considering himself a follower of the classics, he really worked largely on a problem of economic growth, namely income growth and prosperity, and distribution of this growing income between labor, capital and land owners, i.e. between classes. But the central idea of his class theory is the class struggle with a tendency of simplification and polarization of social groups around the main classes of society.

Marx created a coherent and consistent theory, describing the laws of operation and development of the capitalist system of economy. He solved a contradiction that stumped the founders of classical political economy: since the value created by labor alone, the capitalist's profit is the result of the appropriation of the product of workers labor. The English classical school could not explain the origin of profit without finding of a violation of the law of value: if the capitalist buys the labor for operating cost, profit is impossible, if it exists, then work has been purchased below its cost. In other words, the problem was that the worker gets the less value than he is producing by his own labor, and hence does conclude that either the fundamental law of commodity production (equivalent exchange) is violated, or in the creation of value, along with labor there is a participation of other factors.

In Marx's theory the law of concentration and centralization of capital and production plays the important role. By virtue of this law gives small-scale production yield to the large and it is, in turn, to the largest. According to Marx, there is no place for small and medium businesses in a developed capitalist society. But this law implies the inevitability of change of the large-scale capitalist ownership to the public property. The 'vulgar economist', in Marx, is a spokesman of the bourgeois class ideology and because of this, even without the intention to be untruthful, is not able to interpret reality objectively.

There are three main points in Marx' attitude towards capitalism. The first one is that Marx believed the capitalism is inhuman. Even though capitalism is "an immense step forward for mankind, permitting, as it does, an unprecedented expansion of the species-powers" (Elster 1985: 515) in fact "it has disastrous effect for the all-sided development of the powers of the individual human being" (Elster 1985: 515). Second, Marx considered capitalism a profoundly unjust system. As in Marx' point of view "each should receive proportionally to his contribution, assuming his ability to contribute" (Elster 1985: 516), which totally was not a feature of capitalist society as it was already explained above. Third, Marx considered capitalism "inherently and needlessly irrational and wasteful" (Elster 1985: 517) and the capitalist system "tends to destroy itself" (Elster 1985: 518).

The historical significance of Marxism has been and remains associated with activities of large numbers of people - proletariat, interests of which were protected and expressed by this social theory. The ultimate goal of Marxism is designing and theoretical justification for the release of enslaved humanity. Marxism proves the inevitable abolition of all slavery, humiliation, exclusion and lack of freedom of people.

Weber and Marx' comparison

Often one can find the claim that Weber, trying to refute Marx, explained the process of economic development by the impact of religion. Essentially the idea of Weber lies elsewhere: he wanted to prove that the behavior of people in different societies can be understood only within the general theoretical understanding of their existence, where the religious interpretation is only part of the vision of the world. Hence, to understand the behavior of people of different social groups and, in particular, their economic behavior, it is necessary to address the religion as well, although religious perception of the world was in the sociology of Max Weber self-sufficient and self-contained value.

In this regard it seems to be a valid point of view of those researchers of Weber's works, who believe that his work "The Protestant Ethic and the Spirit of Capitalism" does not contain any direct approach to problem of causal explanation; it only deals with the dependence between religious commandments and self-discipline of secular behavior. Weber's thesis on this subject says that there is a clear adequacy of the spirit of capitalism and the spirit of Protestantism. Analyzing the problem of industrial capitalism with its rational organization of free labor posed by Weber, it is possible to draw a few parallels between the notions of capitalism by Karl Marx and Max Weber.

Interpretation of Marx and Weber differ by the fact that the latter considered bureaucratic rationalization as the main feature of modern society and capitalism which cannot disappear, whatever the form of the ownership of the means of production would be. Weber, referring to the collectivization of the means of production under socialism, in difference from Marx has not seen any indigenous transformation. In his point of view, the need for rational organization to get the cheapest product will exist regardless of the revolutions, which determine the nature of the state ownership on the means of production. Weber did not give the decisive role to the conflicts between workers and entrepreneurs and did not believe in the necessity of the class struggle for the establishment of modern society.

Alike Marx, Weber talked about the typical organization of a modern production, which was not happening anywhere except the West. However, he considered the opposition between socialism and capitalism meaningless as the bureaucratic rationalization, as the basis modern society, survives in any mode of ownership. Moreover, Weber, on the basis of the system of individualistic values, was concerned with the development of the collectivization of production, its socialization, which was capable to limit the discretion of the individual. Significant differences between Weber and Marx are to be found in understanding of the nature of social structure and social conditions of society stratification.

Conclusion

In this paper there was presented a brief overview of Marx' and Weber's understandings of the notion of 'capitalism'. It is noticeable that as authors considered capitalism as a phenomenon from slightly different points of view, particularly Weber's perspective is more ideological and cultural, while Marx' majorly deals with capitalism from economic and sociological perspectives. One should also take into account the fact that these sociologists lived in different time frames, so it is upon one's reflection whether Marx would have some arguments to oppose Weber's perception.

References:

Elster, Jon 1940- (1985): Making sense of Marx. Cambridge Cambridgeshire: Cambridge University Press.

Lwith, Karl 1897-1973 (1993): Max Weber and Karl Marx. London: Routledge.

Marx, Karl 1818-1883 (1990): Capital a critique of political economy. London: Penguin Books in association with New Left Review.

Weber, Max 1864-1920 (1996): The Protestant ethic and the spirit of capitalism. Los Angeles, Calif.: Roxbury Pub. Co.

YOUR KNOWLEDGE HAS VALUE

- We will publish your bachelor's and master's thesis, essays and papers

- Your own eBook and book - sold worldwide in all relevant shops

- Earn money with each sale

Upload your text at www.GRIN.com
and publish for free